Collectable Paper Money

GUIDEBOOK WITH COLLECTING TIPS

HOW TO COLLECT
WORLD BANK NOTES AND BANK CHECKS
(COLLECTING BANKNOTES & CHEQUES)

ALAN ACKROYD

LEGAL DISCLAIMER

ISBN-13: 978-1505820270
ISBN-10: 1505820278

Adeptican Publishing

Printed in the United States of America

CONTENTS

ACKNOWLEDGMENTS

Special thanks to Robert Ackroyd for editing, proofreading and composition advice. I also wish to thank some of the estimable paper money specialists of Britain and North America including Colin Narbeth, Yasha Beresiner, Milt Blackburn, Philip Phipps, Jane White and many others for personally helping to enlighten me on the nuances of notaphily and the fabulous world of paper money in decades past. I hope we will meet again soon!

INTRODUCTION

Congratulations on your interest in the world's most exciting collecting field! This book explores some of the most important aspects of this amazing hobby. It shares hundreds of tips, pointers and insights that will help to maximize your enjoyment.

This hobby has been growing in popularity for many reasons. For one thing, it has become increasingly easy to find interesting and attractive banknotes from around the world with great visual, historical and cultural appeal for under a dollar apiece! A banknote collection can be an unbeatable conversation piece and a fantastic investment. Many notes have been growing dramatically in value - some by 1,000% or more within a few years!

Seasoned collectors worldwide, pay big money for single rare notes that could once be acquired at face value. Sometimes this will be to fill a gap in a collection. Sometimes it will be as an investment. Sometimes it will be with a view to passing the item on to a fellow collector or dealer, for an even higher price.

The sums being paid out for rare notes are increasing! For example an American $1,000 note of 1890 could be once bought for $1,000. One of these notes sold for $11,000 in 1970! It sold again in 2014 for **$3,290,000!** A similar note is illustrated in this book. Banknotes are a field where real bargains and amazing profits can be made when you know what to look for - and this book reveals much about this.

As the internet brings the world into closer communication, it becomes increasingly useful to be familiar with exotic cultures and their histories. It is amazing how much knowledge of this kind you absorb when collecting world paper money. It teaches volumes about economics, politics, graphic art and more.

Of course, people also love banknotes for their visual appeal. Besides being a fascinating historical record, a banknote collection is a collection of exceptionally fine artwork. Extensive work and skill goes into the design of banknotes by artists and engravers of exceptional talent. Banknotes display some of the finest engraving and graphic design in the history of mankind.

American Civil War - Confederate States note

The design and manufacturing process is a field of study in itself. Some of the methods are shrouded in secrecy to make forgery as difficult as possible. Nevertheless, forgeries occur, and collectors pay high prices for the better examples.

As collectables, banknotes have some distinct advantages over both coins and stamps. Compared to a coin, a banknote is extremely lightweight and thin, making a large collection much easier to store and transport. Over the postage stamp, the banknote has two sides, and a much larger surface area with more room for interesting information and artwork.

Many stamp and coin collectors are now turning to banknote collecting as the promising new frontier.

The hobby holds many of the same pleasures as stamp and coin collecting. One gets the same thrill at finding that elusive item to fill a gap in a series or a set. There is the same reverence one feels for owning something that has been preserved in perfect condition for a hundred years. There is the same satisfaction of travelling to a collectors' fair to hunt down bargains and meet fellow enthusiasts and develop one's knowledge.

Banknote enthusiasts enjoy individualist status because the hobby is regarded as intriguingly different. It has a certain prestige attached to it; people tend to assume that a banknote collector must be wealthy - although this is often far from true. Novices are usually surprised when they learn that countless attractive banknotes can be obtained for less than 50c each! The hobby also has a refreshing dignity. The banknote collecting fraternity is generally an honest, friendly community, with the genial camaraderie born of a common interest.

The ever-growing availability of cheap and varied material from around the world has brought the hobby within reach of those with tight budgets. This is one collecting field where prices actually fall in many areas, mainly where new issues are concerned. For this, we can thank the effects of inflation. In comparison to the countries of Western Europe and the United States, many countries have had steep inflation, causing their currency to sink in value drastically. Thus, their currency notes become ever cheaper to buy. Some typical cases from recent decades include Brazil, Peru, Argentina, Russia, Afghanistan, Zaire, Iraq, Yugoslavia and Turkey. Consequently, we can even obtain notes with denominations of 50,000,000,000 or more for a dollar or two! Germany and Hungary for example, both suffered runaway inflation in the early 20th century, rendering their banknotes about as valuable as the paper they were printed on in some cases.

Another exciting source of very cheap notes in recent decades was the new ex-Soviet republics. Here was an opportunity to obtain the very first issues of several new republics for mere pennies.

For under $1 each, you can obtain some beautiful, older notes from the early 1900s, the golden age of banknote design. Even notes from the early 1700s can still be bought for under $10 - the 'assignat' notes of the French Revolution, for example.

A collection of paper money is a powerful conversation piece which systematically arouses intrigue, fascination and awe!

Conventions & abbreviations

Throughout this book, I have used the British spelling of 'cheque' rather than the American 'check' to reduce misunderstandings. Under the prevailing U.S. rules of negotiability, a check is understood to be a demand instrument, and some common and less strict American usage of the word 'check' might include reference to an acceptance draft. In this book, the word 'cheque' is interchangeable with the American English 'bank check'. However, my use of the word 'cheque' is used loosely to cover more than one type of monetary instrument, including bank drafts, pay warrants, and similar instruments that resemble bank cheques.

Some of the banknotes illustrated in this book have a reference number indicated such as P103 or PS100. The 'P' is an abbreviation for 'Pick', being the surname of Albert Pick, who was the original editor of the world's foremost value-guide to world paper money, the *Standard Catalog of World Paper Money* (Krause Publications Inc). Albert Pick is no longer the editor, but the prefix 'P' before a numerical reference number is still used to indicate that the number is from the *Standard Catalog of World Paper Money*, which, throughout this book is abbreviated as 'SCWPM'. 'PS' before a reference number indicates that the

banknote is listed in the SCWPM *Special Issues* volume. The SCWPM consists of three volumes in total: Volume 3 covers modern issues, from 1961 onwards. Volume 2 covers general issues prior to 1961 (mostly issues from national banks) and Volume 1 covers special issues: regional banknotes, private and commercial bank issues and so on.

Scottish private bank noteof 1963 depicting the Forth Rail Bridge

1951 note of French Indochina (now Viet Nam)

Cambodia (Kampuchea) 1970s 1000 rial note

Hungarian note of 1941

Disney dollar - legal tender at Disney World, Florida, USA

1
COLLECTING STYLES UNLIMITED

One of the great things about notaphily (the hobby of collecting paper money) is that there is so much freedom to choose how and what you are going to collect. Many newcomers start out without much of a plan, and greatly enjoy a free style of collecting, acquiring any items that happen to appeal to them for whatever reason. Indeed, many collectors never waiver from this style of collecting, while others sooner or later start to specialize in one or more areas. A carefully formed collection with a strong theme can become a historical treatise of great value. If its theme elicits the interest of circles outside the banknote collecting community, this can increase its value further.

If you decide to form a thematic collection, it will certainly have continuity. However, collections that don't have a theme can also have continuity if each group of notes within the collection logically leads to the next in some way. Alternatively, you can develop more than one thematic collection simultaneously. If your existing collection is a free-form one, you have the option of reorganizing it into several separate collections, each with its own theme. If you wish, you can keep one collection free-form, for items that don't fit in with your chosen themes.

There really isn't much that can be written about free-form collecting, except 'anything goes'! So the rest of this chapter is devoted to thematic collecting.

Wildlife is a popular collecting theme.

Collecting themes
and areas of specialization

(1) Collecting notes of a single country

Advocates of this approach enjoy seeking out as many varieties of signature, serial number, and watermark as possible, for each issue. They soon become quite authoritative about the banknotes and other facets of the history of their chosen country. Countries which have produced a proliferation of different banknotes include Russia, USA, China, Canada, and Germany.

(2) Collecting notes from a specific group of countries

North America, South America, Europe, British Commonwealth, ex-Soviet republics, French colonies, Caribbean islands, Africa, S.E. Asia, and the Middle East are all popular candidates. Other types of collecting criteria might include all English-speaking countries or all Spanish speaking countries, or perhaps all countries of the Northern or Southern Hemispheres.

(3) Collecting within a specific historic period

WW1, WW2, 18th century, 19th century, German inflation period, postwar, and the American Civil War are some possible choices.

(4) Collecting by pictorial theme

Illustrations on banknotes abound. The range of themes is vast. Popular ones include monarchs, political figures, animals, birds, flowers, religion, national costume, bridges, forts, refineries, dams, craftwork, agriculture; and nautical, aeronautical, scientific, industrial and military subjects.

(5) Collecting notes produced by a specific printer

The most famous and prolific banknote printers have been Bradbury Wilkinson & Co., Thomas De La Rue, Waterlow & Sons, the American Bank Note Company, the Canadian Bank Note Company, Giesecke & Devrient. These companies have all produced notes for several countries besides their own, so this particular theme can result in quite large collections.

(6) Collecting notes of a specific type

Here are a few of the many possibilities:

(a) Military issues

These can include military payment notes, such as those issued by both the British and American armed forces, from WW2 onwards, for use in occupied areas and military bases. In addition to these, there are the Allied Military issues used for general circulation in several countries at the end of WW2, such as France, Germany, Italy and Japan.

(b) Emergency notes

Individual towns, in countries suffering the ravages of hyperinflation, have resorted to printing their own local currency. This generally happens when the depreciation of the national currency becomes so out of control that people refuse to accept it in payment for goods and services. In 1923 in Germany, for example, workers paid in multimillion mark notes by the sack-load, would take their wages home and use them as stove fuel, to warm their houses. Meanwhile, local currency, issued by town councils, in the form of notgeld (emergency money) was used for everyday shopping for provisions. Emergency notes were also widespread in Austria around this time. They later burgeoned in Spain, during the Civil War, and later still in the Philippines during the WW2 Japanese occupation.

(c) Private bank issues

Many countries have used banknotes produced by private banks rather than government treasuries. Rich hunting grounds for this sort of material include 19th century USA, 19th century Britain, revolutionary Mexico, China, Hong Kong, Canada, Russia, various

South American countries, Scotland (even to the present day) and Germany. If this area appeals, you will benefit from the *Standard Catalog of World Paper Money,* **Volume 1** which covers this type of banknote.

(d) Specimen notes

These are the samples issued to banks prior to the release of a new design, to facilitate identification and authentication. Typically, the word 'SPECIMEN' in the note's native language appears in bold letters either overprinted or perforated. They have also been used to demonstrate prospective new designs, to expedite the selection process. This type of specimen note is much rarer. Neither kind has any monetary value, except as a collectible. This can, in some cases, make them cheaper to acquire than their legally exchangeable counterparts, especially when it comes to higher denominations.

(e) Advertising notes

Not legal tender, but still sought-after collectables, these notes are produced by banknote printers as advertisements and to demonstrate their security-printing capabilities.

Thomas De La Rue (banknote printers) advertising note (2000)

(f) Error notes

Quality control inspectors aim to prevent misprints ending up in circulation. However, some do slip though the net. Printing errors are varied, including missing signatures, smudged ink, color runs, ghosted images, missing colors, mismatched serial numbers and off-centre printing. The more glaring the misprint, the more desirable, from a collector's standpoint! Another type of manufacturing error is the miscut, such as the 'fishtail' where an angular fishtail-shaped appendage protrudes from the note. This occurs when the corner of the sheet was folded back on itself when it was guillotined. Another is the design error: notes bearing incorrect spelling, punctuation, or other blunders. These tend to be harder to obtain than their corrected counterparts which usually supersede them quickly after the error is discovered. Examples are Lithuania

P47a and P29x, Iceland P38a, Hungary P117x, Cyprus P56a, Gabon P9, India P51b, Russia P35a and France P157x.

(g) Forgeries

While it is no longer a hanging offence to possess a forged note, there are still problems with holding a forged note of one's own country, particularly if it is a forgery of a current issue. Some forgeries have been prolific, e.g., the British white notes forged by the Germans in quantity during WW2, (see below) in an attempt to destabilize the UK economy.

During WW2 Germany forged British notes in quantity, and dropped these from aircraft, hoping to destabilize the UK economy.

(h) Printers' proofs

These are the output of printers' test-runs when printing samples of prospective new banknote designs. Few find their way onto the open market, not the least because few are produced, so there is a rarity factor.

(i) Replacement notes

These originate from a sheet used to replace another that failed the quality control standards during manufacture. They bear a special serial number prefix or symbol such as a star, for identification. Only a tiny percentage of banknotes are replacement notes. They are thus harder to obtain, and cost more to acquire.

(j) Hand-signed notes

There was a time when it was commonplace for issuing banks to hand-sign each note prior to its release. As production volumes increased, this eventually gave way to the printed signature. Nevertheless, hand-signing survived until quite recently in some countries - even into the twentieth century in Brazil, South Africa, Mexico, the Philippines and Scotland.

(k) 19th century notes

Antique paper money can still be found at affordable prices - many for under $20 or so. If such a collection appeals to you, the following countries are a few of the good sources of lower priced items that fit this criterion: Great Britain, France, Hungary, Italy, Russia, USA, Germany, Cuba, Uruguay and several other South American countries.

There is no shortage of possible collecting themes for paper money collectors, thanks to the vast array and wide diversity of material. One could say that the range of possible collecting themes is limited only by the limits of one's imagination. Unusual and original collecting themes can be particularly intriguing and conversation-inspiring.

Provincial banknotes from 19th century England

*Block of uncut $1 bills, hand-autographed for the author personally
by former Unted States Treasurer, Mary Ellen Withrow.
(These notes also bear her printed signature, bottom, left.)*

This one could suit coin and banknote collectors alike!

5 million drachma note of WW2, with ancient coin image

1934 Great Depression scrip from New Jersey, USA

Stunning neo-classical allegorical figures abound.

2

THE C-FACTOR

Whatever motivates each of us to collect banknotes, we all have a common desire: to get value for money. What constitutes a note's real value to us? Most collectors take two things into account:

(1) its estimated future worth in monetary terms
    and
(2) the pleasure it brings us while in our possession.

The latter of these should never be overlooked, for happiness and enjoyment are surely worth more than money alone. In this chapter, I'll suggest a tactic to help maximize your returns in both respects.

Have you heard about contemporary art speculators? They look out for relatively unknown artists they believe may one day become famous. They buy paintings from these artists for a very low price. They then wait until the artists (hopefully) become famous. If this happens, their paintings will command relatively high prices. The speculator will then sell their paintings, making a large profit. One such investor—a particularly successful one—was recently asked how he decides which paintings and which artists to invest in. He replied: "The best art is usually the best investment." I believe the same rule of thumb often applies to banknotes. The most beautiful banknotes do tend to be the most sought-after.

Large and beautiful Austrian note of 1902

A complete novice who decides to speculate on paintings without accumulating considerable knowledge beforehand, would be inviting financial ruin. The majority of aspiring artists never attain fame or fortune. However, if that same novice were to collect banknotes instead of paintings, he would be largely eliminating the risk. The reason is that usually only the work of the finest graphic designers ever finds its way onto a banknote. (There are of course the rare exceptions, such as the Mafeking Siege notes, mentioned later.) When a new banknote is ordered, several accomplished banknote designers usually tender their designs, and from these, only one is successful. So by collecting banknotes, it is inevitable that we end up with a collection of fine art of the highest order!

The magic desirability factor

One of the main reasons that banknotes appreciate in value is that they become increasingly hard to obtain after production ceases. Some however, as mentioned above, increase in value more quickly than they would if scarcity were the only consideration. These are the notes with a high C-factor. What is the C-factor? It is a term I have coined to describe special qualities some banknotes possess which typically make them rise in value faster than normal.

The 'C' in 'C-factor' abbreviates the word 'classic'. C-factor notes are those notes that are, or have become, the real classics. The C-factor is in some ways what you might call 'the wow-factor', but it's not necessarily quite the same thing. Hence the need for the alternative term 'C-factor'. C-factor notes usually bear graphical content which gives them almost universal popular visual appeal - to the general public as well as to seasoned banknote collectors. They sooner or later become the notes that everyone wants - the "classics" (hence the C-factor). Consequently they become scarce more quickly than normal.

If we could always predict which notes are destined to become the classics, and buy them while they are still cheap, we would all have some particularly interesting notes that are also fine alternative investment. So how do we identify notes with a high C-factor, early, before they soar in value? It's not always easy; sometimes quite unexpected ones end up becoming classics. All we have to go on is our own common sense, our hunches and our knowledge of what has happened in the past. On looking at the classic notes of the past, I think we can identify certain properties that are usually present in these classic notes. A list of these properties follows (not necessarily in order of importance). It should also be noted that sometimes, if present in sufficient degree, one or two of these properties may be sufficient to promote a note to 'classic' status:

(a) The quality and attractiveness of the artwork.

(b) The popularity, importance, or newsworthiness, of the graphic subject matter.

(c) The singularity of the pictorial subject matter

(d) The singularity of the general appearance.

(e) Its propensity to excite or inspire the viewer due to it beauty, sensationalism or controversy.

There follows some illustrations of examples.

1899 USA Silver Certificate with famous Indian portrait

Cuba P107 bearing Che Guevara's portrait.
Value: around $10.00

USA P337 stunningly impressive neoclassical design
of the American Bank Note Company. Value: around $5,000

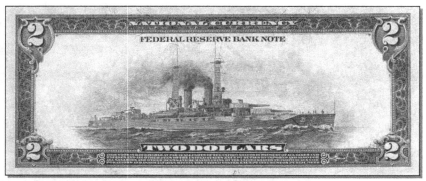

1918 United States $2 Federal Reserve Note
depicting the WW1 battleship USS New York. Value: around $800

Bhutan P12 - exquisite oriental design. Value: around $2.00

Beautiful Spanish note depicting Queen Isabella I of Castile and King Ferdinand II of Aragon, married in 1469

All the above notes were once cheap to obtain. A few of them still are! While the hope of finding profitable gems is always appealing, the main motivator for many collectors is not a quick profit, but rather the adventure of collecting, the pride of ownership and educational intrigue of the hobby. Many lasting friendships are boorn of a mutual interest in the hobby.

Particularly attractive Hong Kong $1 note of 1954

Canadian note with King George V portrait, 1923

American Civil War military scrip

Costa Rica PS174 10 Colones note of 1901 with exceptional train engraving

3
BANKNOTES OF SPECIAL INTEREST

Conversation-inspiring banknotes

Certain banknotes attract special attention, even from the layman who has no prior interest in collecting. A banknote collection interspersed with such gems can make an exceptional conversation piece. Such notes can be surprisingly affordable, such as the examples below.

Specimen notes

Specimen notes are the scarce sample-notes printed with the same methods as the issued version of the note, but solely for issuing to banks for identification purposes. They usually bear the word 'SPECIMEN' (of the equivalent word in the language of the note's nationality). They are sometimes punch-cancelled rendering them irredeemable at face value.

Specimen banknote of the Mexican Revolution, 1914

Banknotes of the French Revolution

French Revolution assignat of 1793

Many of the black and white assignat notes of the French Revolution can still be obtained for under $10; even half that amount if below VF condition. Some of these are quite small in size. The usual dating system is interesting. Many of them bear, starting with 'Year 1 of the Republic'. Also worthy of mention is the currency unit. Most of the assignats were issued before the franc was introduced and were either in sols, livres or sous. It may be of interest that after the revolution, the assignat notes were backed by land confiscated from the church

World War Two banknotes

3rd Reich Winterhilfswerk scrip

WW2 banknotes tend to inspire conversation, but some more than others. Two British notes of special interest are the ten shilling note and the one pound note, which were produced in unconventional colors during the war to make enemy forgeries more difficult. The ten shilling note was printed in light purple or mauve and the one pound in blue and brown. It was the larger white notes that did get forged by the Germans in large quantities with the intention of toppling the UK economy. They were extremely convincing forgeries, right down to the paper and the watermark.

Some of the crude hand-printed notes of WW2 Japanese-occupied Philippines are interesting. Some of them are among the most crudely manufactured paper money you will find. Guerrilla factions, evading capture by the Japanese occupiers lay low in the jungle for the duration of the war. Many of them issued emergency paper money. Typically, the plates were made of lead from discarded batteries, or carved from wood or rubber tire casings. The paper was typically obtained from brown paper bags or old documents.

The occupying forces imposed a death penalty on anyone found in possession of these notes. Many bore the words: 'Payable After the War'. Now that's positive thinking! And of course, it came true; those in circulation were honored at face value by the Philippine Government after the war.

Spain used postage stamps on cardboard discs
as currency during the civil war.

Unusual emergency notes

Emergency notes often take unusual forms. Wartime notes have been produced using crude materials and hand-penned designs such as many WW2 Philippine guerrilla faction notes and notes produced during the Mafeking Seige of 1899. Postage stamps for have been used in Russia, Spain, Austria and Germany. Some of the German ones used in the 1920s are particularly small (20mm square), so it is interesting to have one or more of these as an example of the smallest paper money of all time!

Tiniest of German notgeld

This was the inflation period of post-WWI Germany, during which the national currency rapidly nose-dived in value. Due to the rapid inflation of the national currency, individual towns in Germany started issuing their own emergency money (notgeld).

A great variety of small emergency notes (klein notgeld) were issued throughout Germany and Austria during that period. Many bear interesting pictures and references to local history and folklore. Some of the more unusual examples were those issued by the German fabric-producing town of Bielefeld, printed on silk fabric.

Hyperinflation banknotes

Layman typically marvel when they see banknotes of denominations in excess of 1,000,000. However, a million is mere peanuts in the world of hyperinflation!

1923 Local issue, Bamberg, Germany, 1,000,000,000 marks!

In Germany, the story goes that workers could be seen wheeling their multimillion mark weekly pay home in wheelbarrows, only to burn the notes in their fires as they were worth less than the equivalent weight in firewood. The denominations seen on banknotes climbed to 100 million times one million marks (i.e. 100 trillion marks)! Notes greater than a trillion marks are now scarce, but billion mark notes (1,000,000,000 marks) and even trillion mark notes (1,000,000,000,000 marks) can still be obtained for a few dollars each.

The situation was even more drastic in post-WW2 Hungary. In 1946 at the peak of the runaway inflation, the 1,000,000,000 adopengo note was issued, equal, at that time, to *two thousand million, million, million, million, million pengos*. Now that's inflation!!

Ten Million adopengo hyperinflation note from Hungary

Vertical format banknotes

Many unusual banknotes can be obtained for a few dollars, or less. There are notes printed in vertical format such as the Chinese custom gold unit notes of 1930, printed by the ABNC (American Bank Note Company), and the beautiful 1979 sea life series of the Seychelles whose backs are in vertical format.

Vertical format banknotes from Egypt and China.

Notes made of unusual materials

Notes have been made of unusual materials. Besides the fabric notes already mentioned, some modern banknotes are now being made of polymer plastic. Notes embossed on gold foil were produced in the East Caribbean States in the 1980s. Rectangular 'wooden nickels' were produced in Washington State, USA during a shortage of currency, and another local scrip issue was printed on salmon skin! In Germany, as mentioned earlier, the town of Bielefeld issued local notes made of silk.

German 'klein notgeld' note from Bielefeld, printed on silk

French WWI cardboard currency from Lille, France

Odd shaped notes

Then there are unusual-shaped notes. Spain produced some round cardboard money, affixed with a postage stamp, and there have been square notes, such as the large square 60 baht note of Thailand, issued in 1987 to commemorate Kind Rama IX's birthday.

Thailand 1987 square note commemorating Kind Rama IX's birthday

Square note from Siberia, 1917, printed in the USA by the ABNC

Gigantic banknotes

We've already mentioned tiny paper money. In contrast, how about the opposite extreme? The Russians, in particular, during the early 20th century were keen on very large banknotes. The square note above is just one of many examples. The *Standard Catalog of World Paper Money (Specialized Issues)* lists dozens of them. One of the largest Russian notes is the 500 ruble note of 1912 depicting Czar Peter I.

Superb artwork from the enormous Czarist Russia note of 1912, depicting Czar Peter the Great at left. The complete note is 11 inches long!

There is a similar sized note (200 ruble) bearing the portrait of Czar Catherine the Great.

Accidental design anomalies

Remarkable pictorial features have appeared on banknotes by accident! In Canada, in 1954, people noticed a black devilish face peering out of the Queen's hair on the new banknotes. The design was quickly modified and the accidental demon exorcised.

A famous mishap can be seen in the 50 Rupee Seychelles note of 1968-73. On closer inspection, you may see the branches of two palm trees seem to spell the word 'SEX'. There was no revision of this note's artwork, but it was never repeated.

A 1981 series of Nepalese banknotes was issued with what appeared to be a dark line extending downwards from the King's mouth, giving the impression of dribbling. When this was noticed the notes were reissued with the line erased.

A similar oversight appeared on the 1985 50 baht note of Thailand, on which King Rama IX was depicted with pixie-like pointed ears. The notes were subsequently modified with ear tips hidden!

Spelling errors occasionally appear on banknotes that have slipped through the quality control provisions of various mints. Error notes of all kinds tend to be sought after as collectables.

This Bolivian note has mismatched serial numbers
making it especially collectable and valuable.

Fictitious £1,000,000 banknote from the 1954 movie
'The Million Pound Note', starring Gregory Peck

Collecting has always been in my blood.
—Walter Percy Chrysler

4
CATALOG VALUES

The world's most comprehensive reference work on values, the *Standard Catalog of World Paper Money*, is still referred to by some as the 'Pick' after its original editor, but we'll refer to it here as 'SCWPM'. Its three volumes together list the vast majority of banknotes ever produced - well over 45,000. New editions of each volume are issued periodically to keep abreast of new issues, and changes in the values given in previous editions. The editors do a remarkably good job, considering the large number of banknotes and the diversity of factors that can affect their value at any time. However, the values given are based mainly on the American market, which is one reason why they often seem inaccurate to collectors in Europe and elsewhere. There also seems to be some ambiguity as to what the values represent. They are supposed to represent end-user prices. However, many, especially for some of the very cheap notes, seem clearly to represent the sort of wholesale prices a dealer would pay if he were buying a hundred or more pieces.

Why book values vary

Since banknote values are subject to change, each volume of the SCWPM is most reliable when a new edition has just been published. In particular, this applies to Volume 3 which covers recent issues. However, most experts agree that even new editions usually contain many unrealistic values. To some extent, this is inevitable, because there are many factors that can unexpectedly alter a note's market value. In addition, of course, the catalog editors can only spend a limited amount of time researching each note. Let's consider some of the reasons for the inaccuracies...

(1) Inflation

Some of the wildest discrepancies, particularly with recent issues, are due to inflation in the country of issue. In some countries, inflation is so severe that even if the SCWPM gives an accurate valuation of a note at the time of editing, it is often already wildly out by the time the catalog reaches the collector. Occasionally, inflation can strike suddenly, as in the case of Iraq after the Gulf war. The Saddam Hussein portrait note, Iraq

P73, used to cost collectors around $45. Then when the trade sanctions and other effects of the war took their toll on Iraq, inflation quickly set in. Suddenly P73, together with most Iraqi currency, could be obtained for a fraction of its previous value. Collectors who follow world news and economics have an important advantage: they are better equipped to foresee changes in values, and to judge whether an apparent bargain note really is a bargain - or whether it should be considered with caution.

(2) Demonetization

Here's another thing to watch out for, particularly regarding countries with high inflation: Governments occasionally demonetize a banknote (annul its validity as currency). This happened recently in Croatia. P27 was issued in 1993, and the SCWPM subsequently valued it at $50 in uncirculated condition. A few months later, the Croatian government demonetized it, and suddenly it could be obtained for next to nothing.

Thankfully, this does not often happen. Even so, the more cautious collectors steer clear of countries with high inflation - or limit themselves to buying only the cheapest notes from these countries.

(3) Market Flooding

Occasionally, someone discovers a quantity of a certain note which was previously considered relatively scarce. This happened recently in the case of the Jersey £5 of 1840, PA1. These used to be valued at around $320 in VF. Then, in the early 1990s a hoard turned up, and they could suddenly be obtained for $35 or so. The universal law of supply and demand manifests itself again. As most people know, the more easily available something is, the less one has to pay for it. Consider the air we breathe…

(4) Current Affairs & Market Trends

Prominent political and national events and crises can affect banknote values in either direction. Occasionally something will arouse world interest in a country - banknote collectors included. When a country features prominently in world news, its banknote supply is not affected. The demand however, is. Consider the take-over of Hong Kong by China. The world held its breath, wondering what would become of the region. Collectors anticipated the dissolution of the Hong Kong note-issuing banks. As the big event drew near, collectors worldwide began frantically buying every Hong Kong note they could find, even if they had to pay two or three times SCWPM values.

Later, when the frenzy subsided, banknote values settled down somewhat. However, Hong Kong is still an area of speculation.

(5) Lack of Information

One very important factor to remember is that when the editors of the SCWPM are preparing a new edition, if they have no new data on the current value of a note, its estimated value will remain unaltered. Unless someone draws their attention to an inaccuracy, they have no way of knowing about it.

(6) The American Factor

It is important to bear in mind that the SCWPM is an American publication. Its editors assess the values of banknotes based on their own experience and that of a limited number of dealers, most of whom are based in America, dealing to the American collector. Even so, it is often slow to recognize obvious changes in values and buying trends even within America itself. Confederate States notes, for example continue to appreciate, yet the SCWPM always seems to lag behind in bringing its valuations of these notes up to date. Nevertheless, the SCWPM is undoubtedly more reliable within the boundaries of North America than anywhere else. Let's look at some of the reasons why its values can sometimes be inaccurate for collectors outside America:

(a) National Interests

The USA, like all countries, has its own unique history, its own interests and its own set of friends and neighbors. Banknotes of certain countries are of more interest to the average American collector than, say, his British counterpart. Vietnamese notes, for example, are more popular in the USA, due to the war it fought there. There is evidently more demand in the USA for expensive notes - especially, of course, expensive American notes. For one thing, there are many more wealthy collectors in the USA than elsewhere. When a British dealer chances upon a high-valued foreign rarity, he may offer it at below 'Pick' value if he wants to make a quick sale within Britain. Likewise, you'll find that 'Pick' values for most British notes are generally low compared with the values given in Duggleby's English Paper Money (a British publication reflecting British market values).

(b) Local Availability

Some banknotes are inevitably easier to obtain in the USA than in Europe. Obvious examples are the notes of Canada and Latin America, along with the Bahamas, St. Pierre & Miquelon, Hawaii, etc. Others are harder to obtain there, and the American collector will have to pay more for these than he would in the continent of origin. To some extent, this effect is balanced out by the fact that a country tends to be more interested in the banknotes of its neighboring countries than anyone else is. So although the demand is higher there, so is the supply.

(c) Economies of Scale

Compared to most countries, there are more dealers in the USA, and in particular, more dealers with substantial buying-power. If you are a collector in the USA and you want a certain note, you have a better chance of finding a dealer who has been able to buy a quantity of that note. When a dealer buys in quantity, he usually pays a low price, and is therefore sometimes willing to sell at a lower price. Unfortunately for the European collector, many of these dealers will only sell in quantity also, and will not get involved in small orders - especially if they come from overseas. In any case, when you consider the additional cost and risk of transatlantic delivery, it usually makes sense to pay a little extra and buy from a competitive dealer in your own country.

(d) international differences of collecting ethos

American collectors tend to be keen on obtaining scarce banknotes in the highest possible grade. Collectors from most other countries tend to be less particular, adopting a more relaxed "you get what you pay for" approach. The SCWPM often reflects the American style—especially for high-value notes.

There is no instant shortcut to becoming an expert in assessing the value of banknotes. However, we've covered some of the important factors. The more you learn about banknotes, the economic situations in their countries of issue, and the prices people are paying for their banknotes, the more adept you will become.

Above all, remember: the true value of a banknote is what someone is willing to pay for it - which may not be the same as what some hopeful dealer is asking - or what the SCWPM says!

A hobby a day keeps the doldrums away.

—Phyllis McGinley

5
HOW CONDITION AFFECTS VALUE

A slight difference in the grade (i.e. condition) of a note can often mean a big difference in the value. Therefore, it is important to ensure that your supplier is grading his notes accurately according to strict standards. The correct definition of each grade can be found in the first few pages of each volume of the *Standard Catalog of World Paper Money*, also referred-to as 'the Pick catalogue', after its original compiler.

The standard grades are as follows: Poor, Fair, Good, Very Good, Fine, Very Fine, Extremely Fine and Uncirculated. Of course, a banknote might fall somewhere between any of these grades, so plus-signs are often used to indicate intermediate grades. For example: F+ falls somewhere between F (fine) and VF (very fine). 'A' for 'almost' is also used: 'AEF' means 'almost extremely fine' and 'AU' means 'almost uncirculated'.

Banknote value-guides, such as the *Standard Catalog of World Paper Money* usually give about three different values for each note: usually those for VG, VF and UNC. If you need the value of the note in an intermediate grade, you have to estimate it for yourself, based on the values and grades given. For example: if the following values were given: VG:10.00, VF:40.00, UNC:80.00, it is then a simple matter to estimate the intermediate grades' values: F will be about 20.00 and EF will be about 60.00.

We can illustrate this with a simple graph; the three known values are ringed with small circles.

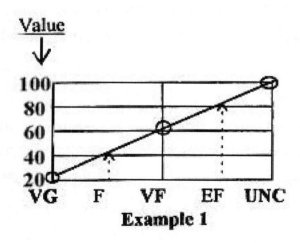

Example 1

Some banknotes are especially scarce in the higher grades. In these cases there will be a much greater difference in value between EF and UNC than there is between VG and F examples. Let's suppose that the catalogue gives the value of a note as being 2.50 in VG, 20.00 in VF, and 100.00 in UNC. We could create another grid - ideally on graph paper - and plot the known values (ringed with the small circles on the grid below). Again, we draw a line passing through the three values in order to be able to read off the values of the intermediate grades. This time, the line has to be a curve, to pass through the points. In this case, the curve gets progressively steeper, the closer we get to UNC.

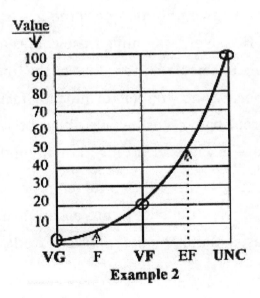

Example 2

In cases like Example 2, a slight difference in grade towards the UNC end of the scale results in a remarkable difference in value. Plotting a graph, such as those above, is one of the easiest and most accurate methods of estimating the values of those intermediate grades not given in the SCWPM. A more accurate way is to use the special online calculation utility called the *Ackroyd-Noteval Banknote Valuation Utility*. This can be found on the World Wide Web.

Only by gaining a good understanding of grading, can you accurately appraise banknotes. The various reference works, such as the *Standard Catalog of World Paper Money* are indispensable aids. Unfortunately, they generally give only two or three grade-values for each note. However, assuming these values are correct, it is possible to calculate the values of the unmentioned grades. There is no simple formula to facilitate this, since different banknotes behave differently in the way they increase in value according to their condition.

Remember that Pick values are sometimes unreliable, even after taking into account the fact that they are based mainly on the American trade market.

Forty defects to watch out for

More than forty defects can debase the value of collectable paper money. A list follows. Notice that 'cleaning' and 'pressing' are included as defects. Any form of processing is regarded as degrading, partly because it cannot be undone. All processing inflicts additional damage to the integrity of paper collectibles. Although some visual 'improvement' may be achieved, the seasoned collector will invariably opt for the unprocessed item that is graded honestly.

Bent corners	Grease marks
Bleaching	Hand stamps
Brittleness	Ink spots
Cancellation cuts	Limpness
Cancellation punching	Loss of sheen
Central wear-hole	Pinholes
Cleaning	Pressing
Corner wear	Printing smudges
Counter's bends	Repairs
Creasing	Rust spots
Discoloration	Skewed printing
Dullness	Soiling
Doodling	Spike holes
Edge nicks	Staining
Edge wear	Staple holes
Fading	Tape marks
Finger marks	Tears
Folds	Trimming
Foxing	Uneven margins
Graffiti	Water damage

Post-WWI German klein notgeld - small-sized regional emergency notes easily distinguishable from the Austrian counterparts (below) by the currency unit which is marks or pfennigs)

Post-WWI Austrian regional notgeld, distinguishable from the German counterparts by the currency units: kronen and heller

6

GETTING TO GRIPS WITH GRADING

For the benefit of newcomers to the hobby, 'grading' refers to the physical condition of an item. Be sure to familiarize yourself with the established grading terms and their meanings. You will discover some of the apparent paradoxes of banknote grading, such as how 'good' really means 'bad', and how 'fair' really means 'awful'!

A clear understanding of the established grading norms is important because a slight difference in condition can mean a big difference in value. This is particularly so towards the high end of the grading scale. For example, the difference in value between an uncirculated note, and the same note that's almost uncirculated, can be as much as 20%. A sound knowledge of grading is your primary defense against the bane of unscrupulous, careless or ignorant dealers.

Your supplier should be grading his items strictly according to the IBNS conventions as described in the *Standard Catalog of World Paper Money*.

Don't be deceived!

The pleasures of buying banknotes are greatly enhanced when we feel we've paid a favorable price. However, it is a fundamental mistake to select your supplier purely on the grounds that his prices appear low, or that he always allows you some discount. It is important to establish whether he is grading his notes accurately. It is remarkable how much opinions differ among dealers regarding how to grade banknotes. A note described as 'very fine' by one dealer, may be only 'fine', according to another. It is crucial to be aware of this, because the jump in value between the successive major grades, G, VG, F, VF, EF and UNC, can be as much as 100%! To assess your understanding of this, consider the following: From which of the sources below, would you buy a banknote from?

(1) Dealer A, who describes it as 'F' at $20.

   or

(2) Dealer B, who describes it as 'VF' at $22, after discount.

The naive collector might immediately jump at dealer B's offer, since it looks a far better deal, because a 'VF' note is often about double the price of a 'F' example. However, if you bought both examples from the two dealers, and compared them, you might find that despite the varying descriptions, each note is identical in grade (say, F+). It then becomes clear that dealer B is giving much worse value than you expected, and dealer A is giving superior value, by $2.

Furthermore, if you had been buying from dealer B over a long period without being aware of this, the sum of the losses from all your purchases might be substantial. If this dealer had been your only supplier since you started collecting, your whole collection could be worth only 50% of what it should be. This would make it virtually impossible for you to recoup your money if you decide to sell your collection within the next few years. So it makes sense to check that you are getting value for money each time you purchase. Thankfully for collectors, English law permits you to return any unsatisfactory item supplied by a mail-order company. If you feel that a note has not been properly described, you should have no qualms about returning it. Of course, you may tend to be forgiving, if the dealer has occasionally sent you notes higher in grade than specified, at no extra charge.

How many grading terms does your supplier use?

As already mentioned, there is quite a big difference in condition, and thus value, between the major grades, G, VG, F, VF, XF and UNC. The differences in value are usually increasingly large towards the top end of the scale. Nevertheless you may have noticed that the majority of notes listed by most dealers, mysteriously coincide with these few major grades alone! This should raise a big red question mark in your mind. The above major grades are only six points on a scale of innumerable nuances of condition. It is therefore plain to see that a dealer who is conscientious about grading should be using many intermediate grading terms. These include: G+, AVG, VG+, VG++, F+, F++, AVF, VF+, VF++, AXF, XF+, XF++, AU, and AU+. If you see a dealer's list, devoid of these intermediate grades, you should ask yourself what is going on.

Question: If a dealer limits himself exclusively to using only the major grades, what happens when a note is midway between, say, VF and XF?

Answer: He is limited to choosing one grade or the other, and the chances are, he will use the higher grade, to make it look like a more attractive offer. If you bought this note, you would find it to be only VF+ or VF++, and therefore worth perhaps 25% less than the price you paid!

The importance of a worded description

Despite the availability of intermediate grading terms to describe banknotes, there are always many cases where the note's condition cannot be fairly described using grading terms alone. To illustrate this, try answering the following: How can the condition of the following notes be properly described, using the standard grading terms alone, where:

(1) a note is perfectly uncirculated, yet it was printed off-centre, so that the margin widths differ wildly.

(2) a note is AU, except for a tiny tear (tears are usually permissible only with the grade F and below).

(3) a note is technically VF, however, it was printed badly, and the colors are dull and unappealing.

(4) a Commonwealth note is VF, except that a doodler has adorned the Queen with an Adolf Hitler moustache.

These are just a few of the innumerable examples of this problem. It frequently occurs with UNC notes. A note should only be described as UNC if its condition has not changed since the moment it left the printing press. However, with some notes, the manufacturing quality varies greatly from note to note. Therefore, in some cases, a technically UNC example could have such faults as unequal margins, rough edges, smudged ink, staple holes, crooked edges, skewed printing, etc. How can you know about such flaws if the dealer is too lazy to provide a worded description? You cannot, and you are almost bound to find that some of the notes you purchase are disappointing. There are of course other obvious reasons why a worded description is useful and helpful.

Important points to remember

(1) UNC means 'as perfect as it was when it left the press'. While an UNC note may have certain slight defects when it leaves the press, these should

never include bends (nor even slight counter's bends).

(2) If a note has been folded so many times that a small hole has appeared where the major folds intersect, the note must never be described simply as 'F'. 99% of these notes should be described as VG. However, where such a note is too perfect to be described as VG, it is permissible to use a description such as: 'small central hole where folds intersect, otherwise F'. Typically this sort of description will be abbreviated, due to space limitations, as follows: 'sml/h fr/fldg, o/w: F'.

(3) A note with edge tears should never be described as anything higher than F, unless the tears are mentioned; for example: '2mm e/tr, o/w:VF'.

(4) XF (also called EF) is an often-abused grading term. According to established grading standards, as described in the Standard Catalog of World Paper Money, an XF note may have one strong crease, or up to three folds i.e., bends that aren't sharp enough to be called creases. Apart from this, the note should be virtually perfect.

(5) Bear in mind that even where a dealer offers a worded description of each note, space may be too

limited to describe all the faults present. In such cases he will generally exercise some discretion when stating grades. For example, a note might have only one strong crease, but it is only a very small one in a corner. The dealer might be justified in describing this note as XF++ or even AU. Another note might have an edge tear, but otherwise it is XF, so he strikes a compromise between F and XF and calls it VF. You should always consider this possibility before concluding you have been swindled.

Four WW1 prisoner of war camp notes from Aschach, Austria

7
DON'T BE CHEATED

The satisfaction of collecting paper money is even greater when you feel you've received value for money. For most collectors, the preferred approach is to find a reliable dealer whose prices are lower than average, and stick with him. However, there are always those occasions when one needs to buy from someone unfamiliar. At those times, you should be particularly careful to check that the note you are buying has been graded and valued correctly. Knowledge and awareness are your best defenses against being cheated - especially when buying in distracting conditions, or when intoxicated with eagerness to buy.

The importance of accurate grading

Picture this: You are perusing the back streets of an unfamiliar town one weekend, and you stumble across a one-day collectors' market taking place in a hotel. You wander inside, just in case there are some banknotes. You notice a coin & stamp dealer in one corner. As you saunter across, you feel a rush of anticipation when you see he has an album of paper money on display. On inspection, the prices seem refreshingly low. You size up the dealer out of the corner of your eye. You conclude that he's a respectable old gentleman doing this as a half-hearted hobby and obviously hasn't bothered to keep his prices up to date.

You browse through the album and see many cheap notes in rather poor condition... nothing very exciting. Then, just as you arrive at the last page, your heart misses a beat and leaps into your throat, where it remains firmly lodged. There, before your eyes, is Bahamas P12b - the very note you've long needed, to complete a series, but have never been able to find (probably because it books at over $1,750 in UNC condition)! Now, at last, you've found one, and the price tag says $100! You pinch yourself to make sure you're not dreaming. Pinch-check confirms waking state. "$100!!" you silently screech to yourself, as your limbs begin to tremble.

Suddenly a group of three other banknote collectors appears by your side, like a pack of hungry wolves who have detected the scent of your excitement. One of them quickly homes in on your discovery and hovers over you, poised to snatch it away from you at the slightest opportunity. You realize it's time to make a quick decision. You ask the dealer if you might take the note out of its holder and examine it more closely. He agrees. The lighting is rather poor, but you can see how perfectly flat the note is - no bends, no creases, no pinholes and nice sharp corners - pristine, mint and uncirculated, just as described!

Despite the note's ridiculously low price, you try your luck to see if you can haggle the price even further in the direction of ridiculous (shame on you)! "Will you accept $85 for it?" you ask. The dealer looks you in the eye, pauses for a long moment, then breaks into a benevolent smile and asks, "Can you pay cash?" By an unusual stroke of luck, it just happens that you have $85 in your wallet. You agree, and count out the money. With great care, you place your new treasure safely between the pages of a book you are carrying and you thank the dealer, shaking his hand vigorously. Feeling ten years younger, you start to make your way home, already visualizing your treasure in its new home in your album.

After arriving home, you settle down to enjoy your evening meal, after which you prepare for the scheduled arrival of a fellow banknote enthusiast who promised to pay you a visit. The doorbell eventually rings and you invite your friend to come in and make himself at home. "I told you should have come with me on that trip today," you taunt. "Look what I found!!" You carefully hand him the banknote, making no attempt to conceal your pride. Your friend's eyes widen. He dons his reading glasses and holds the note up to the light, obviously spellbound. You await his envious comments... "Well, what do you think?" you prompt.

Your friend remains silent for another minute, then turns and looks at you over the top of his glasses. "What do I think?" he repeats, quizzically... "I think you've been cheated! This note is nowhere near uncirculated! It's been pressed!" He's really got your attention now. "That will approximately halve its value." He adds. "In addition to that, its edges have been trimmed to make them straight and to make the corners sharp. That will perhaps halve its value again."

The smile has disappeared from your face. "On top of that, it has a one-inch tear and several pinholes, all of which have been expertly repaired. That will halve its very low value yet again. If that's not enough to ruin your day, it has also been washed!" Then comes the coup de grâce: "And last, but not least, for good measure, it has also been starched to add crispness. Before all this took place the note was only in 'G' condition. It should have been priced at around $30 tops. How much did you pay for it?"

As the last vestiges of color drain from your cheeks, you try to utter some sort of reply, but the lump in your throat allows you only to produce a very audible "GULP"! You look at your watch, but it is already far too late to go back to the market and try to claim a refund - or strangle the dealer.

That is not the end of the story either. You later find out that the note is a forgery! However, before you break out into a cynical chuckle, I should finally add: The forgery turns out to be worth twice as much as the amount you paid! Fate has the last laugh this time; it is your lucky day after all - but only just!

This rather extreme tale serves to illustrate some of the pitfalls awaiting the unwary. Thankfully, only a small percentage of all the notes on the market have been processed in any way. Furthermore, honest dealers will always tell you if a note has been so "upgraded" - provided they are aware of it themselves. Bear in mind also, that doctoring a note in itself is neither a sin nor a crime, except when done with the intention of misleading a buyer. Let's look in detail at the methods used, and the tell-tale signs to look out for:

(1) Washing and cleaning

The purpose of washing or cleaning a banknote is to improve its appearance and increase its value. When carried out by a judicious expert, it can sometimes do just that. Frequently, however, washing is carried out by amateurs who succeed only in diminishing the note's value.

A dealer should always tell you if he thinks a note has been washed or cleaned. Here are some possible signs of a washed or cleaned note:

(a) Limpness

All notes can eventually become limp - usually after they have been reduced to 'G' condition from prolonged use. However, when a note seems more limp than it should be, considering its appearance, this often indicates that it has been washed. VF, EF or UNC notes should have a high degree of crispness.

(b) Loss of sheen

Most banknotes have a pronounced sheen until circulation reduces them to F+ condition or thereabouts. This sheen is most noticeable when observed under an electric light bulb at a certain angle. Washing and cleaning invariably reduces this sheen and often removes it altogether.

(c) Worn, but unnaturally clean creases

The most common method of washing includes the use of a weak solution of sodium chloride & sodium hypochloride which bleaches out dirt and staining. Most notes that have been excessively circulated naturally become dirty, especially along worn creases where the printing ink has worn away. These worn creases are particularly susceptible to bleaching, because the chemical solution can easily act upon the individual fibers of the paper there. If you see a well-used note whose creases look unnaturally white, you can suspect that it has been chemically washed.

(d) Localized Cleaning

Cleaning can also be carried out on a small localized area of a banknote - usually to remove a small stain or graffiti. If you see a note with a very faded, barely visible penned numeral or other writing - it may have been thus cleaned, especially if the area surrounding the graffiti looks unnaturally clean. Various chemicals can be used to remove ink from banknotes. Again, such cleaning is not always detrimental to a note's value, but it can be - especially when carried out by an amateur.

(2) Pressing

This is another means of attempting to upgrade a note. The most common method is to dampen the note, then place it inside an old book with absorbent pages. The book is then laid flat and a heavy weight applied. After 24 hours or so, the note is removed, in perfectly flat condition. In some cases, pressing can improve the appearance of a note, but sometimes it can reduce its value. This often happens with French notes - the type made of very thin paper with a fine embossed texture. These notes often become buckled or wavy due to atmospheric moisture, even though they may be uncirculated. Such surface undulations can be flattened out by pressing the note, but this invariably destroys its crispness somewhat. Most collectors would rather have an undoctored, crisp note with a few surface undulations or bends, than one that is dead flat but without its original crispness. A note should never be described as UNC if it has been pressed.

(3) Repairs

Some skilful repairs can only be seen when examined carefully under a good light coming from the correct angle, or with the aid of a magnifying glass. Such repairs are often carried out using very thin specialist document tape. Pinholes can be filled in with color-matched acrylic paint or similar substances, by anyone with a magnifying glass, a good eye and a steady hand.

(4) Trimming

If you see a note whose edges seem unnaturally clean and sharp, considering the degree of wear to the rest of the note, you should be suspicious. If the margins of the note seem narrower than they should be, you should be doubly cautious. Trimming is often carried out by amateurs (and amateurish dealers) who cannot even cut straight. The original cutting, usually done with a mechanical guillotine, is always dead straight. Consequent trimming - perhaps with a sharp knife and a rule is rarely as straight. However, do bear in mind that some older notes were cut by hand in the first place - often very inaccurately. Some were even torn apart, rather than cut. Also, if you see a note with margins of unequal width, you should not immediately conclude that it has been trimmed, because notes often turn up that have been accidentally printed off-centre.

Only a small percentage of notes have been processed in any way. Even so, a safe strategy is to buy from a reliable dealer whenever possible, bear in mind the above points, and always examine your purchases!

Repairing at it's most drastic! - a note made by splicingtogether the top halves of two indentical notes!

8

STORING AND DISPLAYING

The pleasures of collecting paper money are enhanced when you have a well organized, good quality system for storage and display. Having a good storage system enables you to relax, knowing that your collectibles are safe from environmental harm, such as boisterous kids, clumsy adults, spilled drinks, ultraviolet light and other damaging factors. Caring for your collection will preserve its value. Presenting it to best effect can actually increase its value.

Caring for your collection

Remember that the difference in value between a choice uncirculated note and an almost uncirculated example can be as much as twenty percent, so it makes sense to take great care of your collection -

especially those uncirculated notes. Let's list some precautions you can take.

Protect your notes with the right kind of clear plastic. The chemicals in some plastics can wrinkle, exude chemicals and damage your notes. The best policy is to use only a purpose-made leaf, designed for housing valuable paper items.

Use a good quality ring binder. Some are supplied with a useful protective slipcase. These add significant protection, especially when your collection is being moved around.

An alternative form of storage is to house each note in its own clear plastic sleeve. This is the method used by most dealers. This method offers the greatest scope for easy reorganization. An album, however, seems to make a more attractive coffee-table conversation piece, and is generally considered more pleasing to browse through. If you go for the sleeve option, you will need suitable boxes to hold them. If the boxes are just the right size, it will help to keep the sleeves neatly stacked, one behind the other, vertically. You may even be lucky enough to find a chest of drawers with small drawers just the right size. Before the days of computer databases, chests like these, made either of wood or metal, were once widely used in offices for holding large index cards.

Handle your notes with care. Merely dropping one to the floor can reduce its grade from 'uncirculated' to 'almost uncirculated', if it lands on its corner. Obviously, handling a note with dirty or greasy hands or allowing a young child to get hold of it are the sort of things to avoid. Bear in mind that even careful handling causes some damage, albeit on a microscopic level. Enough careful handling will eventually degrade the note's condition visibly. Human skin produces oils which attract dirt and otherwise degrade your notes. Therefore, it makes sense to carefully wash and dry your hands before handling them.

Avoid leaving paper collectibles under bright light or sunshine. This can cause the colors to fade after a while. Avoid storing your collection in a damp environment. This can help the growth of molds and bacteria that can result in foxed or otherwise discolored notes. It can also cause buckling of the paper. Avoid accidents! Keep pens, cups of coffee and unattended toddlers well away from your banknotes. Always look out for other potential hazards in the immediate environment.

The worst thing that can happen to your collection is total loss, through theft, for example. Most collectors like to ensure that their collections are covered under their household contents insurance. But even if yours is, I am sure you would prefer not to have it stolen! Luckily banknote collections are not often stolen, because they are not easy for the average burglar to liquidate. They also bear serial numbers - and it is an excellent idea to draw any potential thief's attention to this. You might stick a plaque on the inside of the front cover saying, in bold lettering, "All serial numbers have been recorded for security purposes". You might also draw the potential thief's attention to the fact that the notes are obsolete (and therefore cannot be cashed in at a bank). Another idea is to put a label on the spine of the album saying "Family Photos", or suchlike. What burglar is going to take time out to peruse your family snaps?

Presenting your collection

Besides preserving the value of your collection by taking care of it, you can actually add to its value - without waiting around for the notes to appreciate! How? By displaying it to best effect.

This is another good reason for using a quality binder. Banknotes stand out beautifully if they are placed against a dark background. If you cannot find a supplier of ready-made interleaves, you may consider making your own. One way to make them is from single-pocket leaves, with a sheet of black or dark colored paper inserted into the pocket. You might want to use a dark navy-blue paper to 'set off' a trio of notes with predominantly blue colors, or a very dark brown paper to compliment a group of notes with predominant tans and ochres in their color schemes. You can also use the backs of the insert to mount cuttings or annotations referring to the notes on the following page. Then each time a leaf is turned, the viewer is presented with an appealing double-page spread, with the notes on the right, and relevant texts, or neatly-written annotations on the left - everything nicely accentuated by a contrasting dark background.

Having the notes always displayed on the right side only, also adds effect, because it helps to focus the viewer's attention. If you have, say six or seven notes all displayed at once, the eye has difficulty knowing where to settle, and when it does, it is more likely to be distracted by the other notes all vying for attention. The main purpose of the interleaves, are of course to stop the notes in the next leaf from being visible, and to ctreate a contrasting colored backdrop to make your notes stand out.

Hand-written or typed annotations can greatly enhance your collection, especially if you explain something about some of the notes that isn't immediately obvious. The portraits and illustrations on banknotes are often without explanatory text. This gives you the opportunity to supply the missing information for your viewers. It is best to be as neat as you possibly can. If you are writing by hand, it is best to use a top quality pen, and use it throughout. If your handwriting is untidy, you had better have it typed, or written by a friend who excels at calligraphy.

We mentioned attention to detail. One of these details is cleanliness. Repeated leafing through an album may soon leave fingerprints and dust on your pristine super-clear leaves. Polishing them with a clean, soft cloth will eliminate these and restore that pristine sheen to your display. When displaying your notes in albums, pay attention to detail. If you have a leaf with three pockets, each containing a note, do your notes justice, and place each one centrally, with absolute precision.

Occasionally, people like to frame banknotes, and certainly many of them can be displayed to great effect this way. If care is taken during the framing process, there is no reason why the notes cannot one day be returned to a collection in the same condition as they were before framing. Probably the best way to hold the notes in place against the backing is to use clear photo corner-mounts. You stick these to the mounting surface, so each corner of the note slips into its own corner-mount. Naturally, you will want to ensure that the finished item will be hung somewhere beyond the reach of sunlight. Some people even go to the trouble of using glass that filters out UV light.

Paying attention to all these tips can result in a collection that really impresses people - even though some of the notes only cost you 50c each! It will also ensure that your collection is safe from damage, so that it can pass through the years unscathed. Hopefully, in fifty or eighty years' time, your UNC notes will still be just as they were when they left the printing press. Who knows how many people down the line will benefit from your efforts. Hopefully they will all be as careful as you.

British Armed Forces notes, issued for use at British military bases

9
MONEY-SAVING
OPPORTUNITIES

Collectors often ask for advice on what to buy. Since no two collectors are the same in what they want from the hobby, it is usually difficult to be specific. It is easier to give general advice on how to get value for money - and that is advice most people appreciate. It is so much more satisfying to buy a banknote or cheque when you know you are getting it for a low price. For one thing, this means that you stand a better chance of selling it at a profit, if ever you decide to sell. Bear in mind, however, that no matter how experienced you become, there will inevitably be occasions when you lose out. Even the shrewdest collectors, dealers and investors get it wrong sometimes. If you can live with that in mind, you should find that the rewards of collecting greatly outweigh the occasional pitfall. Indeed, many collectors derive an exquisite pleasure from this hobby, unmatched by any other activity.

Getting value for money, checklist

(1) Buy from a trustworthy dealer whose prices are known to be on the low side.

(2) To maximize your chances that the note will appreciate in value, accumulate experience of the market. The more you learn, the more you will be able to recognize a note that is likely to appreciate fast, through increasing scarcity and demand.

(3) Seize upon opportunities to buy cheaply when they arise. Have a fund of money set aside for such opportunities if you can.

(4) Be certain that the condition of the item is as described. Minor variations in condition can mean substantial differences in value. So check the note very carefully - even if it came from a reputable dealer. If it turns out to be below the described grade, you can haggle for a lower price.

(5) Once you have acquired a note, do take meticulous care of it. Handle it as little as possible. Protect it from the dangers of theft, moisture, bright sunlight, smoky air and clumsy, sweaty or dirty fingers. Even when it is safely housed behind plastic, it is advisable to handle with care.

Where to bypass dealers and buy at face value

Sometimes there are opportunities to buy at particularly low prices - face value, even! For example, your local high street banks can be a valuable resource, if you collect British paper money. It is worth mentioning to your favorite bank clerks that you collect obsolete banknotes. Ask them if they ever receive any from their customers, and if it would be possible for you to buy them. With luck, they will remember to set some aside for you. People often come in with the older one pound and five pound notes of various dates. They even occasionally come in with old white five pound notes, asking if they can still cash them in! While you are there, you might ask them if they have any unwanted specimen banknotes or specimen travelers' cheques.

The bureau de change

If you collect modern world paper money, there is one source of material you should not forget. It's your local bureau de change or foreign currency exchange. Almost every major town has at least one. The leading travel agents often have one in their main branches.

American Express has foreign currency outlets in many towns and cities.

You can profit from such establishments if you approach them in the right way and build a friendly relationship with their staff. Think about it. They hold hundreds of foreign banknotes, some of which may be just what you need for your collection. If you buy them from a foreign exchange bureau, you'll be paying face value only, plus the agent's commission.

Here's how it went for me. One day I walked into a bank in my town and saw a Thomas Cook foreign exchange counter. There was a queue there so I went away and came back later. Bank clerks are less inclined to give some 'eccentric' collector personal attention when there are 'proper' customers waiting in line! When I went back, there was no queue, and the lady was idly shuffling papers, and probably deciding what to cook for her evening meal. I casually strolled up to her and when she looked up, I tentatively asked her if she had any mint condition foreign notes in her drawer - or for that matter, anything unusual - explaining that I was a collector. She appeared quite happy to check through the wads of foreign notes. At that time, there were quite a few European notes that could easily be obtained in UNC condition from France, Greece, Germany, Holland, and Italy. Most of them I already had, so I asked her "Do you have any British Commonwealth notes there - especially ones with Queen Elizabeth on them?" There was nothing there on that occasion, but I did not come away empty-handed. She produced some Portuguese notes that were virtually uncirculated, yet were not the current issue. I paid her face value plus a $2 commission, and came away with about five of these notes that, as collectors' items, were worth at least twice what I paid.

Every time I went into town, I'd drop into that bank. I developed a friendly rapport with the two people who usually worked behind the counter. On my third visit, one of them even suggested I make a list of any particular countries I was looking for, and give it to him so he could look out for them. Since then, he has occasionally telephoned me to tell me that one of the items on my list has arrived, and was I interested? On another occasion, his colleague called me in his own time, and said he'd just got back from a holiday in South America, and had brought back some paper money that I might like.

Surprisingly, these bureaux de change sometimes hold old, obsolete notes that are worth more than face value. People come back from holiday with foreign notes still in their wallet. They make a mental note to change them back to English money, but they never get around to it, until perhaps a couple of years later, by which time those notes have been superseded by a newer design.

Foreign banks

If you ever go abroad yourself, you have a great opportunity to obtain some foreign banknotes at even lower prices - directly from the foreign banks. It is easy to walk into a bank and ask one of the tellers if she has any perfect unused banknotes. And while you are there, you might as well ask if they have any specimen notes they don't want. You never know your luck. Of course you will need a good command of the local language to get all this across without having them silently label you as just another insane foreigner!

Unless you are the sort of semi-active collector who is content to collect only the odd note acquired cheaply from such sources, you will usually find yourself having to pay a banknote dealer full market value for your notes. However, all is not lost, because many banknotes are growing rapidly in value. I feel very satisfied when I consider how little I paid for certain notes a few years ago - even though I paid the full market price.

Auction houses

If one of your goals is to build a collection that will appreciate in value, it is generally a good strategy to base your collection on quality rather than quantity. Pick scarcer notes, in the highest grade possible. A little experience will teach you which notes are the scarce ones. They are the ones that are rarely offered for sale.

It would be wrong to assume that every scarce, expensive, high grade note will appreciate fast. The two factors that cause a note to appreciate are scarcity and demand. You have to study the field in order to get a better idea of what is genuinely scarce and what is in demand - and what is likely to be in demand in future years. Never jump to any hasty conclusions about this. The more you learn, the more likely your purchases will appreciate, given time.

If you are interested in high-value scarcer notes, you might consider investigating some of the up-market numismatic auctions. Spink & Sons, and Phillips (both in London) hold regular banknote auctions, and will gladly send you their catalogs, if asked. You'll find notes valued at hundreds - even thousands - of pounds each. Even if you never place a bid, their illustrated catalogs can be quite educative - especially when you study the list of prices realized at previous sales. If you do decide to bid, you stand a chance of obtaining some sought-after notes at low prices. There is a lot to be said for deciding upon a maximum bid, prior to the sale, and sticking to it - no matter how strong the temptation may be to outbid someone else, during the actual sale. Remember to take into account any commission and VAT that may be added by the auctioneer (read the terms of sale). It is usually wise to bid only for items you have actually viewed, prior to the sale. If you have never attended one of these auctions, you might find it quite an eye-opener. Collectors and dealers from diverse countries fly over specially to attend them. You may witness some amazingly high bids that will stun you, when you consider that all notes were once available to collectors at face value.

Never forget the cash machine!

The possibility of picking up a rarity for a tiny fraction of its real worth is one of the attractions of banknote collecting. Recently, someone in London, England obtained a run of £10 notes from a cash machine, all with the serial number, AA 000000. They changed hands a few days later for no less than £650 each! (Hardly surprising, since this sort of serial number is normally found only in royal collections, etc.) It is always a good idea to check the notes issued by cash machines, because they are usually uncirculated, and have been loaded without having been individually checked, except by the banknote printers' quality control system, which time and gain has proven fallible. Printing errors do slip through the net, and these are always worth more than face value to a collector. The more obvious and bizarre the error, the better! Cutting errors are equally collectable and valuable, the worse the error, the higher the value! Serial numbers are always worth checking because the scarcer and more interesting number combinations such as, say, 987654321, or 656565656 or 7777777, or low numbers like the ultimate 0000001 will be bought for a high premium by the right collector. Even mildly low numbers can be worth more than face value. Always check your notes for unusual serial numbers!

British ten shilling note of the 1960s (notice the valuable serial number)

1950s British £1 note, 1950s;
these are still occasionally handed in at UK high street banks

10
INVESTING IN PAPER MONEY

The performance of obsolete banknotes, as an alternative investment, has been astounding in recent years. In past decades, stamps and coins have attracted speculators, but many are now turning to paper money for the big returns. The rewards are enhanced by the ever-growing number of collectors attracted to paper money for various reasons: For one thing, a banknote has a large surface on which attractive artwork and information of historic interest can be displayed, and unlike stamps, both sides are attractive. Unlike coins, they are colorful. They are also lightweight, making them easier and less expensive to store and transport.

As with all commodities, the values of collectable banknotes are affected by availability and demand. This principle works to our advantage because each new banknote design is produced in limited numbers only. After production ceases, it becomes increasingly hard to obtain, as supplies are either destroyed, degraded or bought up by collectors. As collectibles, they then become increasingly sought-after, partly because the number of collectors is growing, and partly because collectors are keen to obtain items that are getting scarcer and growing in value.

Amazing profits being made

One doesn't have to look far for recorded examples of the remarkable profits that have been realized by banknote investors. In 1986 a speculator bought some rare 1933 Australian specimen notes for £1,404 (UK£) each, at Christie's in London. A few months later, the same notes exchanged hands in Australia for about $52,000 (AU$). More recently, four of these specimen notes - one of each denomination - were valued, as a set, recently at $180,000 (AU$). That's about £69,000 (UK£), representing an increase in value of over 4,800% in thirteen years. In 1989, another investor purchased an American 1863 $1,000 Treasury note for $121,000 (US$). It was a note commonly nicknamed the 'Grand Watermelon' due to the coloring and appearance of the large zeros on the reverse. The same item was sold, nine years later for

$792,000 - a profit of $671,000 or 554%. In 1982, an investor paid $1,550 (US$) for a Hong Kong $50 from the Bank of India, Australia and China, in XF condition. These now fetch around $45,000 - an increase of over 2,800%. In 1984 the Australian 1932 £10 note in VF condition had a catalogue value of $275 (US). One of them was sold recently for $11,800.00.

Dwarfing all the above, was the recent purchase of an American 1890 $1,000 "Grand Watermelon" for an amazing $3,290,000 in 2014! The same note was purchased in 1970 for mere $11,000. Witness the phenomenal investment potential of some banknotes!

A "Grand Watermelon" sold for $3.29 Million at auction in 2014!
(The portrait is of Civil War General, George Gordon Meade.)

All of the above cases made the news because of the sums of money involved, but most profits are made on much cheaper notes, every day of the year. The more common examples of Confederate States bank notes of the American Civil War could be bought for about 25c in the 1940s. Nowadays these notes fetch around $50, an increase of nearly 20,000%! On the collectors' market, uncirculated banknotes often rise to many times their original value within a few years after they become obsolete.

Be aware of course, that past performance is not necessarily a reliable indicator of future performance, and not all banknotes perform the same!

Historic events can arouse a sudden interest in certain notes, thereby driving up the value. For example the adoption of the Euro currency by eleven countries in 1999 triggered a sudden increase in demand for the pre-Euro national currency notes of Austria, Belgium, Finland, France, Germany, Ireland, Italy, Luxembourg, the Netherlands, Portugal, and Spain. Be aware however, that historic events can sometimes inflate a note's value only temporarily. This happened with Hong Kong recently. When the British handed it back to China in 1997, there was fervent speculation over Hong Kong banknotes and for a while they sold for two or even three times book value in many dealers' lists, but shortly thereafter, the values receded back almost to where they were before the hand-over—because Hong Kong remained remarkably unchanged despite Chinese rule. Even so, many shrewd investors anticipated the rapid rise in value of Hong Kong notes and made a quick profit by buying early and selling at the right time.

Indeed, timing is one of the keys to success. It is important for judging when to buy and when to sell, but also for judging when to get involved in the collecting field in the first place. There's much to suggest that now is the time to get involved in the field of paper money, because it is still young and unexploited compared to coin and stamp collecting.

Besides good timing, another key to success is of course to buy at a favorable price. Then you are off to a head start. If you buy a note at 50% of market value, and sell immediately at market value, you've immediately made 100% profit. You may of course choose to hold the item in anticipation of further appreciation.

While some historic events create a short-lived rise in the demand for certain notes, bigger events can cause a more sustained interest. World War II banknotes continue to be in hot demand even 70 years after the event, and even among generations born since that era. And the interest is rife in many countries, because so many countries were involved. When speculating on a banknote, it is wise to consider (a) how long it is likely to be particularly sought-after and (b) by how many people. If a note is sought after by a lot of people from many countries, for a long time, this will have a greater affect on the banknote's long-term appreciation than if the demand is only short-term, among the collectors of a single country. However even the interest of a single country can have a significant effect if it's a country with a lot of affluent collectors.

So there are many factors to consider when estimating which notes will perform best. The more knowledge you can absorb about international current affairs, economic conditions and trends in the banknote collecting world, the better equipped you'll be to make successful choices. But in the final analysis, you'll also have to rely largely on logic, common sense and sometimes instinct. Beware of buying notes that are still in circulation when the country in question has an inflation rate exceeding that of your own. But with obsolete notes, you are usually safe. Most obsolete banknotes rise in value over time, in a more or less steady manner. Of course, some rise faster than others, and it is the speculator's task to try to pick the ones that will appreciate the most.

In most cases you will need to hold a banknote for a reasonable length of time to realize a worthwhile profit. For example, after 10 years most banknotes have shown a marked growth in value, and the well-chosen ones a more substantial increase in value. When you have decided on a note you want to buy, for investment purposes, it's generally best to buy it in the highest grade you can find (or afford) - if possible, 'uncirculated' (i.e. as pristine as it was when it left the printing press). Then preserve its condition with impeccable care, because even a slight bend, crease or other blemish will knock a significant percentage off a previously 'uncirculated' note's value. Banknotes can always be degraded, but never up-graded. Therefore, the uncirculated examples become increasingly scarce.

The SCWPM (*Standard Catalog of World Paper Money*) the three heavy volumes produced by Krause Publications Inc., USA, is the reference work which most collectors of world notes use for guidance on values. The reference numbers assigned to each note therein are now used worldwide. It is updated at regular intervals, but be aware that the publishers are often slow to register changes in value of many notes, as any experienced dealer will confirm. This is hardly surprising when there are some 50,000+ banknote designs that have been produced worldwide since the invention of paper money (attributed by many to medieval Chinese merchants).

The SCWPM is an indispensable asset for anyone involved in collecting or speculating on world banknotes, despite the inaccuracies. No-one will deny that weather forecasts are frequently wrong, yet no-one will deny that weather forecasts are better than no weather forecasts. More often than not, though, the values stated in the SCWPM are reasonably accurate. And if you can buy the new editions every time they are issued, you will soon have a valuable reference with which you can observe trends, and the changing value of any individual note - at least to the extent that the changing value has been recognized by the publishers.

Besides the *Standard Catalog of World Paper Money*, publishers in several countries produce value-guides specific to their own country: Great Britain, USA, Germany, Hong Kong, Portugal, Italy, Canada, and Yugoslavia, to name a few. These country-specific catalogues are often more accurate in their valuations than the SCWPM.

Dealers are often better informed about a specific note's true market value than the publishers of the catalogues are. So by talking to dealers you can often find out that certain notes are becoming scarce before, say, the SCWPM has recognized it. However, dealers too can get values wrong - and this can work in your favor; it means there are usually bargains to be found amongst their stock.

One opportunity the speculator can profit from, is when the value of a note is temporarily deflated. This can happen occasionally when a hoard of some note is discovered and released onto the market. A recent example was the Jersey white £5 note of 1840. This used to catalogue at hundreds of pounds due to its scarcity. Then in the 1990s a hoard came onto the market. Immediately the value dropped to about £30 in XF condition. The SCWPM took some time to recognize it. The size of the hoard is relevant. If the hoard is really big, it may be a long time before the fresh supply is absorbed by collectors so that values are driven upward again. In the early 1990s, a very large hoard of obsolete British Armed Forces notes was unleashed on the market. These notes, previously hard to obtain, suddenly dropped in value, wildly.

Finally, when thinking about the returns you will get from any banknote investment, consider that the monetary profits are only one way you may benefit. Don't discount the excitement of speculation, and the pride of ownership of scarce, coveted, often stunningly beautiful items of great historical interest which make exceptional conversation pieces. In fact, rather than lose sight of your investments forever by selling them, you may well decide to pass them on to a child or grandchild, who can reap even greater rewards in years to come.

The best intelligence test is
what we do with our leisure.
—Dr. Laurence J. Peter

11
IDENTIFYING THE COUNTRY OF ORIGIN

Collectors occasionally find it hard to determine the nationality of a banknote. It is easy to determine its nationality when its country of origin is printed on it in English, or in a language using western characters, where the spelling is similar to the English spelling; for example, Türkiye (Turkey) or Moçambique (Mozambique). There are however a number of countries whose banknotes aren't so easy to identify.

Nationality identification chart

For that reason I have included the section below, illustrating the country-identification panels of banknotes that typically leave the average westerner confused. I hope you will find this to be a useful identification aid.

Armenia

Bangladesh

Belarus

Bosnia Herzegovina

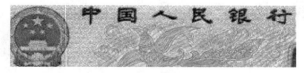

Bulgaria

China

Estonia

Georgia

Japan

Korea, North

Korea, South

ҚАЗАҚСТАН

Kasakhstan

КЫРГЫЗ БАНКЫ

1 БИР СОМ

Kyrghyzstan

Laos

МАКЕДОНИЈА

Macedonia

Бүгд Найрамдах Монгол Ард Улс
УЛСЫН БАНК

Mongolia

Nepal

NORGES BANK
betaler mod denne Seddel
til Ihcendehaveren
FEM KRONER

Norway

Russia

NÁRODNÁ BANKA SLOVENSKA

Slovakia

BANKA SLOVENIJE

Slovenia

SVERIGES Riksbank

Sweden

Tajikistan

Thailand

Transdnestria Republic

Ukraine

ЎЗБЕКИСТОН

Uzbekistan

WW2 banknotes

12
KNOW YOUR WORLD CURRENCIES

How many different currencies are there in the world? Quite a few! Some readers may be surprised at the length of the following list. It is not always easy to identify the origin of a banknote. One important clue is the name of the currency unit, which is often stated on the note. As a banknote identification aid, below is a list of the main world currency units of recent years, and the countries which have used them.

List of world currencies

ADOPENGO: Hungary

AFGHANI: Afghanistan

AUSTRALE: Argentina

BAHT: Thailand

BAISA: Oman

BALBOA: Panama

BIPKWELE: Equatorial Guinea

BIRR: Ethiopia

BOLIVARE: Venezuela

BOLIVIANO: Bolivia

CEDI: Ghana

CENTAVO: Cuba, Guatemala, Nicaragua, Philippines

CENT: China, Sierra Leone, USA

CENTESIMO: Uruguay

CENTIME: Saar

COLON/COLONES: Costa Rica, El Salvador

CORDOBA: Nicaragua

CRUZADO, CRUZEIRO, CRUZADO NOVO: Brazil

DALASI: Gambia

DENAR/DENARI: Macedonia

DINAR/DINARA: Algeria, Bahrain, Croatia, Iraq, Jordan, Kuwait, Libya, Sudan, Tunisia, Yugoslavia

DIRHAM: Morocco, United Arab Emirates

DOBRA: St. Thomas & Prince Islands

DOLLAR: Antarctica, Australia, Bahamas, Belize, Bermuda, Brunei, Canada, Cayman Islands, Cook Islands, E. Caribbean States, Fiji, Grenada, Guyana,

Jamaica, Liberia, Malaya & British Borneo, Namibia, New Zealand, Rhodesia, Singapore, Solomon Islands, Trinidad & Tobago, Tuvalu, USA, Virgin Islands, Zimbabwe

DONG: Cambodia, Laos, Vietnam, S.Vietnam

DRACHMA: Greece

DRAM: Armenia

DUCAT: Moldavia

EKUELE: Equatorial Guinea

EMALENGENI: Swaziland

ESCUDO: Chile, Mozambique, Portugal

EURO: Some European Union countries

FEN: China

FLORIN: Aruba

FORINT: Hungary

FRANC: Algeria, Belgium, Benin, Burkina Faso, Burundi, Cameroon, Chad, Comoros, Congo, Djibouti, Equatorial African States, France, Gabon, Guadeloupe, Katanga, Luxembourg, Madagascar, Mali, Martinique, Monaco, Morocco, Niger, Rwanda, Saar, Senegal, Switzerland, Tahiti, Togo, Tunisia, West African States

FRANCO: Equatorial Guinea

FRANCS GUINEEN: Guinea

GOURDE: Haiti

GUARANI: Paraguay

GULDEN/GUILDER: Netherlands, Netherlands Indies, Netherlands Antilles, Surinam

HELLER: Austria

HRYVNI/HRYVEN: Ukraine

INTI: Peru

JEON: South Korea

JIAO: China

KAK: Cambodia/Kampuchea

KARBOVANTSIV: Ukraine

KINA: Papua New Guinea

KIP: Laos

KOBO: Nigeria

KORUN: Czechoslovakia, Czech Republic, Slovakia

KRONEN: Austria, Bohemia, Romania

KRONER: Denmark, Norway

KRONOR: Sweden

KRONUR: Iceland

KROONI: Estonia

KUNA: Croatia

KWACHA: Malawi, Zambia

KWANZA: Angola

KYAT: Burma/Myanmar

LARI: Georgia

LATI/LATU: Latvia

LEI/LEU: Moldova, Romania

LEK/LEKE: Albania

LEMPIRA: Honduras

LEONE: Sierra Leone

LEVA: Bulgaria

LILANGENI: Swaziland

LIRA/LIRE: Italy, Turkey

LIRA/LIROT: Israel

LIRI: Malta

LITAI/LITAS/LITU: Lithuania

LIVRE: Lebanon

LOTI: Lesotho

MAKUTA: Zaire

MALOTI: Lesotho

MANAT: Azerbaijan, Turkmenistan

MARK: Bosnia, Germany, Saar

MARKKA: Finland

METICAIS: Mozambique

MILPENGO: Hungary

MILS: Cyprus

NAIRA: Nigeria

NAKFA: Eritrea

NEW PENCE: United Kingdom (military issues)

NEW SHEKEL: Israel

NGULTRUM: Bhutan

NGWEE: Zambia

NOUVEAUX MAKUTA: Zaire

OUGUIYA: Mauritania

PA'ANGA: Tonga

PATAKA: Macao

PENCE: Falkland Islands, St. Helena

PENGO: Hungary

PESETA: Spain

PESO: Argentina, Bolivia, Chile, Columbia, Cuba, Guatemala, Guinea-Bissau, Mexico, Philippines, Uruguay

PESO ORO: Columbia, Dominican Republic

PIASTRE: Cambodia, Laos, and Vietnam, Egypt, Sudan

PISO: Philippines

POUND: Biafra, Cyprus, Egypt, England, Falkland Islands, Guernsey, Isle of Man, Jersey, Lebanon, Libya, Nigeria, Rhodesia, South Africa, St. Helena, Syria, England, Scotland, Northern Ireland, Isle of Man, Jersey, Guernsey

PULA: Botswana

PUNT: Republic of Ireland

QUETZAL: Guatemala

RAND: South Africa

REALES BOLIVIANOS: Bolivia

REICHSMARK, RENTENMARK: Germany

RIAL: Iran, Oman, Yemen

RIEL: Cambodia/Kampuchea

RINGGIT: Malaysia

RIYAL: Saudi Arabia, Qatar

RUBLE: Russia, Tajikistan, Tatarstan

RUBLEI: Belarus

RUBLI, RUBLU: Latvia

RUFIYAA: Maldives

RUPEE: Ceylon, India, Mauritius, Nepal, Pakistan, Seychelles, Sri Lanka

RUPIAH: Indonesia

RUPIE/RUPIEN: German East Africa

SCELLINI, SHILIN: Somalia

SCHILLING: Austria

SHILINGI: Tanzania

SHILLING: Biafra, Kenya, Somaliland, Tanzania, Uganda, England, Isle of Man

SHEQEL/SHEQALIM: Israel

SOLES DE ORO: Peru

SOM: Kyrgyzstan,

SUM: Uzbekistan

SUCRE: Ecuador

SYLI: Guinea

TAKA: Bangladesh

TALA: Samoa

TALONAS/TALONU: Lithuania

TAMBALA: Malawi

TENGE: Kazakhstan

TOLAR/TOLARJEV: Slovenia

TUGRIK: Mongolia

TURK LIRASI: Turkey

VATU: Vanuatu

TYIYN: Kyrgyzstan

WON: North Korea, South Korea

XU: Vietnam, South Vietnam

YEN: Japan

YUAN: China

ZAIRE: Zaire

ZLOTYCH: Poland

13
CHEQUE
COLLECTING
BASICS

Cheques are still a relatively undiscovered field of paper money collecting. However, this branch of notaphily is rapidly gaining in popularity, due to its obvious attractions for anyone who appreciates handsome old documents, financial history, elegant handwriting, and collectibles that grow in value. Now is the time to get into cheques while they can still be obtained at incredibly low prices due to the hobby being largely undiscovered by the collecting public.

A much-overlooked collector's treasure trove

In some senses you get more for your money. As I write, attractive 19th century cheques will cost you perhaps one tenth of what you would have to pay for an equally attractive banknote of the same period! Yet each issued cheque is unique due to the hand-written element. No two issued cheques are identical, because the hand-entered details vary from cheque to cheque.

Assistant Treasurer of the US cheque, 1850s - fabulous design for this period, setting the trend for subsequent decades.

Background information

English law defines a cheque as: 'a bill of exchange payable on demand'. A normal bill of exchange, however, is usually payable on a specified date, sometime after the day it was issued, thus affording the issuer a period of credit. They are usually written on the issuing company or individual trader rather than a bank. They are much less common today. A cheque, on the other hand, is usually written on a bank and is payable 'on demand' to the payee (unless it's a 'bearer cheque' which is payable to anyone who acquires it).

It's worth noting that the law does not insist that a cheque has to be written on a pre-printed cheque form such as those that banks supply in cheque books. Cheques have been written on scraps of paper and in one case, on a pair of lady's underwear which passed through the clearing system and was eventually paid! *The Guinness Book of Records* holds that the strangest cheque ever issued was one that was written on a cow!

Cheques have been around at least since Roman times. In the middle ages, the Knights Templar pioneered international banking when they started issuing promissory notes (forerunner to the bank cheque) to pilgrims and continental travellers. A traveller could thus deposit money with the Templars in one location, and retrieve it from Templars in another location within Europe and beyond. The traveller thus became relieved of some of the danger posed by bandits and robbers en route.

In the 1600s, the goldsmiths (in effect, the nation's bankers) issued receipts for gold received. These goldsmiths' notes circulated freely as paper money, eliminating the need to convey actual gold, and were the forerunner of the modern cheque. Cheques became more common in Britain with the spread of the provincial banks in the 1700s and more prolific with the development of the postal service and electronic communications in the 19th century. Pre-printed cheque forms first appeared around the mid-1700s.

There is certainly no shortage of material. In the 19th century there were many hundreds of independent provincial banks in Britain. Over the years, pairs of these amalgamated, until today when we have little more than 'the big four' whose branches we find in almost every high street. A collection of cheques can form a poignant record of banking history. The names of the numerous banks and the banking family trees are subjects too vast for this short chapter. However, your local main library may provide an excellent starting point for research.

British cheques are often visually impressive, especially the large company cheques (e.g., 9.5in x 5.5in or bigger) that came into fashion in the early 20th century. However, if you want cheques with interesting pictorial elements, the USA is hard to beat. Starting in the 1800s, it has been common practice in the US to incorporate one or more pictorial elements into a cheque's design - or in the case of modern examples, a picture in the underprint. Some of the more elaborate examples of yesteryear were produced by great security printers such as the ABNC (American Bank Note Company).

Handsome Nevada State Treasurer's warrant
of the gold rush era, with railroad & mining vignettes

Adding to the appeal of older cheques, are the duty stamps many of them bear. These represent a collecting field on their own. As the hobby stands, you often don't have to pay a premium for a cheque with a scarce duty stamp. Yet you end up with a collection of duty stamps within a collection of cheques - and possibly for no extra charge! Nevertheless, an unusual duty stamp can add considerable value to a cheque. These revenue stamps took the form of adhesive stamps, but later designs were printed directly onto the cheque. The American examples of these were often a large and elaborate, usually printed as an orange underprint, many incorporating a president's silhouette.

Another attraction of older cheques is the exquisite handwriting many of them bear. In centuries past, beautiful refined handwriting was the norm. It is largely a lost art today, due to the development of printing technology and word processors. 19th century cheques, particularly from Britain and North America often bear the most beautiful cursive writing, replete with fabulous flourishes akin to the exquisite 'round hand' penmanship of Britain's George Bickham the Elder (1684–1758). In the latter half of the 19th century, Spencerian script took over to a large extent in North America, but this also took on some beautifully flourishing forms.

Handwriting reached the pinnacle of its beauty in the 1700s to 1800s in the days of steel dip pens and ox gall ink. For those who appreciate the art, the cheques of the 1800s are a good place to find stunning examples.

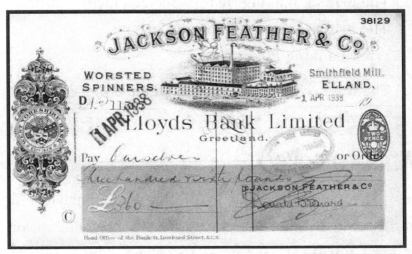

Large pre-WW2 British company cheques like this one have wide appeal.

On an older cheque, you are more likely to find the signature of a prominent member of business or government. Researching the name of the signatory can often turn up some remarkable facts. If you can say a few interesting words about the signatory, you will add value to the item. But it's not just the signatory that is worthy of research. Each old cheque you acquire is a clue to an amazing jigsaw puzzle of hidden history.

To enrich your experience of this hobby there are societies you may like to join. As a member, you will typically receive a periodical journal with news and articles on the hobby. Here are a couple:

(1) The British Banking History Society, incorporating The British Cheque Collectors Society: www.banking-history.co.uk

(2) The American Society of Check Collectors: www.ascheckcollectors.org

What to collect

The field of cheque collecting is extensive and multi-faceted. Newcomers are often overwhelmed, or at least unsure, about what to collect. The hobby is relatively new, with no set rules or conventions. How you collect, and what you collect, is limited only by your imagination and personal inclinations. However, here are some popular approaches:

(1) Free-form collecting

Some collectors prefer complete freedom to collect anything that can be described as a cheque. Others will also include travelers' cheques, bills of exchange, sight notes, bank drafts, money orders, certificates of deposit, pay warrants, promissory notes etc. However, some people feel that such free-form collecting leads to an unsatisfying and chaotic 'accumulation' rather than a manageable and serious collection. These people prefer to limit their intake, aiming for quality over quantity. Hence we see more specialized collecting styles such as the following...

(2) Collecting by area

Collectors sometimes restrict their focus to a limited area, such as their home town. This can be an intriguing approach, as it invariably uncovers amazing hidden facts about the town's history. Beware that unless your town is a big one with a rich past, you may find yourself enduring long periods waiting to find suitable items for your collection. You can remedy this by expanding your area of interest to the boundaries of your county - or your overall region. For American cheque collectors the area of interest could be one or two of the major cities or a particular state. The North Eastern States, especially New York and Pennsylvania, provide the richest pickings since they were the most industrialized and populated during the 19th century.

(3) Collecting by period

Collectors sometimes concentrate on a particular period of history: the 18th century, the 19th century, WW1, WW2, the inter-war period, the American Civil War, to name a few possibilities.

(4) Collecting by pictorial theme

British cheques have a special elegance and appeal, but few bear pictorial elements. American cheques, on the other hand, often bear interesting pictorial vignettes. Popular pictorial themes for collectors include: bank buildings, trains, ships, eagles, Indians, sailors, historic portraits and allegorical figures such as Liberty. If you want more freedom you could, of course, collect ANY cheque that bears a vignette or other pictorial element.

(5) Collecting by company theme

Company cheques are often more elaborate and visually interesting than the personal variety. They are prolific of course, so collectors often limit their area of focus to specific types of company. This especially makes sense in the case of American cheques, because the size of the nation and its rich commercial history, provide such a rich hunting ground. Company types favored by cheque collectors include mining companies (especially gold and silver), railroad companies, canal companies, and famous manufacturing companies such as Coca Cola, General Motors, etc.

(6) Travelers' cheques

This variety of cheque went through a colorful and elaborate period in the 1960s, and it can be interesting to collect such cheques bearing the names of banks which are still in business today.

British travelers' cheques, 1960s and 70s

(7) International banks

There was a time when London was the international banking centre of the world: definitely the basis for an interesting cheque collection. Every prominent British bank has branches overseas, and every significant foreign bank has, or had, a branch in London. The cheques of these international banks, besides being interesting in themselves, often bear numerous hand stamps applied by various overseas banks. This is also true of travelers' cheques.

(8) Collecting items of a specific bank

Many banks have, or have had, numerous branches nationwide (or state-wide in the case of US banks). Setting out to acquire one cheque from each branch that has ever existed is an interesting challenge. Collectors often seek every example of the bank's logo, monogram or imprint, as developed over the years.

Regarding the above collecting themes, remember that you do not have to limit yourself to any one theme. You can develop more than one thematic collection simultaneously. This helps to eliminate frustrating periods when no suitable additions can be found. If you are still unsure what to collect, why not try a starter pack, which many dealers will be willing to provide you with at low cost.

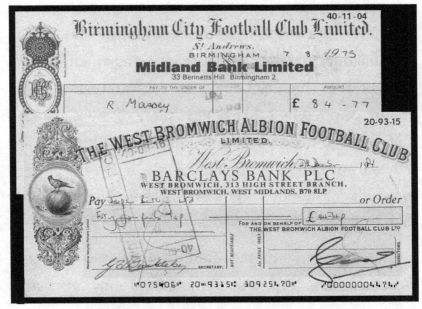

British football club cheques of the 1960s & 70s

Where to obtain collectable bank cheques

The most fruitful and best-organized sources are usually specialist dealers. It helps if your supplier bothers to describe each item in detail in his catalogue. Then you have a much better idea of what you are buying. Other sources include ephemera auctions and paper money collectors' fairs, where you have the advantage of being able to examine and, hopefully, cherry-pick the goods before buying. Then you can secure optimum value for money by picking out examples that are in the best condition, and/or those that bear the most elegant handwriting and/or an unusual duty stamp that is not obscuring an interesting part of the cheque. Look also for interesting hand stamps applied by other banks; some of these are rare and add significant value. Remember too that earlier dates are usually the most desirable. It always pays to look out for famous signatures. Sooner or later, you may well get lucky.

If you get into the hobby now while it is still largely young and unexploited, and buy attractive interesting items at what seem like sensible prices, there is every chance that your collection will multiply in value as the sources of these items dry up. Still, it always pays to get a head start by obtaining your cheques at the best prices possible.

Pre-1900 American cheques with interesting vignettes

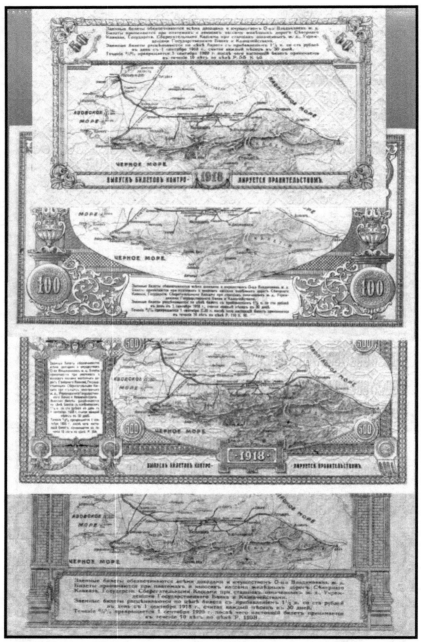

1918 Russian 5.4% interest-bearing Black Sea Railway loan notes of the
Vladivkaskav Railway Co., each bearing a map of the Caucasus rail route
from Rostov-on-the-don to Petrovsk and Baku on the Caspian Sea

14
PAPER MONEY TERMINOLOGY

Collectable paper money glossary

Allied military currency

Currency issued for use by the allied forces at the close of WW2. Used by the British, US, French, Russians and others.

Assignats

Notes issued during and after the French Revolution, backed by land confiscated from the church.

BAF notes

British Armed Forces Special Vouchers - paper money issued for use only within British military bases.

Bearer cheque

A type of cheque payable to whoever possesses it, rather than to a specific person or organization. They have occasionally served as currency, passing hands between successive payers and payees, until someone cashes it in.

Block numbers

A number printed on a note, indicating the specific printing run. Not the same as the plate number or serial number.

Broken bank notes

The term is usually applied to the notes from the many US banks which became insolvent during the mid 19th century.

Cancellation

A method used by authorized bodies to cancel a note's monetary value. Methods include hole-punching, signature removing, overprinting, etc.

Colonial currency

British sterling notes issued in North America from 1760 to the American Revolution.

Commemorative

A note bearing reference to a historic event, person or organization - usually issued on the anniversary of a major event of national significance.

Demonetization

The official cancellation of a banknote's validity as currency, by government decree.

Depression scrip

Paper money issued by private organizations during the American depression of the 1930s, as an alternative to currency. It was redeemable in cash or goods, as specified on the note.

Emergency issues

Notes issued during times of economic turmoil, usually when the country's national currency approaches worthlessness, or as a substitute for coins when metal is in short supply.

Error notes

Notes with design errors such as spelling mistakes and notes with badly-printed features or other manufacturing faults. They are sought-after as collectibles.

Fantasy note

A novel or humorous banknote look-alike with no monetary validity, often with a make-believe denomination, and sometimes portraying a celebrity or fictional theme.

Grade

The physical condition of a banknote; the degree of wear and tear. A minor difference in grade will have a significant effect on value.

Guerrilla notes

Paper money issued by guerrilla organizations, during enemy occupation of their country. These were commonly used during WW2 in the Japanese-occupied Philippines.

Guilloche

Embellishment found on some banknotes - a motif of intricate interweaving lines, created by a mechanical engraving machine, like an elaborate spirograph.

Hell money

Fantasy notes from China, used in funeral rites and other rituals, where they are offered as a symbolic sacrifice.

Intaglio printing

Printing method using an engraved metal plate. Oil is applied to the plate. Ink is then applied. Due to the oil, this only adheres in the engraved grooves. The plate is then pressed onto the paper, where the ink held in the grooves transfers onto the paper.

JIM notes

'Japanese invasion money'; banknotes issued by Japan during WW2, for use in the countries it occupied.

Mules

Mules, or mule notes, are bank notes that have been printed using mismatched printing plates. For example, the plate number on the front of the note is different from the one on the back, as in the case of certain United States bank notes.

Notgeld

A German word meaning emergency money. German and Austrian notgeld abounded in the early 1920s inflation period.

Notaphily

A word that someone coined to mean 'bank note collecting'.

Political notes

Banknote look-alikes printed with political messages or propaganda, often bearing a portrait or caricature of a newsworthy person or politician.

Provincial notes

Notes issued in the UK by provincial banks independent of the Bank of England, prior to 1923.

They were common in the 19th century. Also used to describe notes issued by provincial governments in Canada.

Remainders

Notes which were printed but never issued. They sometimes lack authorizing features such as signatures, dates etc.

Replacement notes

Notes cut from a sheet used to replace any sheet in a print run that failed to pass the quality control standards. They can be identified by their special serial number prefix. They are invariably more valuable than the normal banknotes due to their relative scarcity.

Reprint

A note printed from the original plates, usually long after the note has become obsolete. These are somewhat collectable and should not be confused with ordinary reproductions, which are not printed using the original plates.

Security features

Devices incorporated into banknotes to make forgery difficult, including foil security threads, micro-text, special inks, and silk threads imbedded in the paper.

Serial number

The consecutive numbers printed on successive banknotes during a print run, using a numbering machine, to give each note a unique identity.

Shinplasters

Colloquial term for small-sized notes; in particular, American fractional notes.

Siege notes

Emergency notes issued by besieged bodies; for example, during the sieges of Mafeking, Khartoum, and Parma Nova.

Silver certificates

U.S. bills which were redeemable in silver until 1968. They bear the legend 'Silver Certificate', as opposed to 'Federal Reserve Note', for example.

Skit notes

Banknote look-alikes with a political, satirical or humorous theme.

Specimen notes

Demonstration notes for private distribution to banks, etc., for identification purposes, just prior to the release of a new series. They are printed with the same equipment as the real item, but carry no monetary validity. To indicate this, they are usually overprinted or perforated with the word "SPECIMEN" in the language of the issuing country.

Star notes

US *replacement notes* that bear a star-prefixed serial number.

State notes

United States bank notes issued by individual state governments in the 19th century.

Test notes

Test notes are used for testing ATM machines etc. They imitate the size and weight of the genuine banknotes, but are printed with designs significantly different from the real notes. Some bear the words 'TEST NOTE'.

Vignette

An isolated pictorial feature on a banknote, cheque or other monetary instrument.

A vignette

~END NOTE~

I hope this brief excursion onto the fabulous field of collectable paper money has refreshed your appetite and provided some useful insights. Of course, we have only scratched the surface of this extensive hobby, but we have covered some of the most important aspects and provided clues about some of the many avenues of exploration that are open to you.

The exhilarating intrigue of this hobby becomes most evident when you visit a major banknote collecting fair. Most western countries hold at least one every year. Attending a major banknote fair with a shopping list is one of the great thrills of this hobby. If you do this, it's highly advisable to take the latest edition of the *Standard Catalog of World Paper Money* with you. This can be obtained at **www.aanotes.com**. Then you will have much better idea of whether the prices being charged for any particular note are reasonable. Who knows, I might even see you at one! If you see my name on a name badge, please say hello; I would be glad to meet you.

If you are not already a member, do consider joining the **International Bank Note Society**. A link to this organization may be found at the web site below, which is also a place where you can contact the author:

WWW.AANOTES.COM

Thank you for buying this book. If you enjoyed it, please give it a good rating at the seller's online outlet, and please recommend it to your collecting colleagues.

Best regards ~ Alan Ackroyd

This concludes our guided tour through the wonderful world of notaphily. For further information you may like to visit the Author's paper money website:

WWW.AANOTES.COM

Printed in the USA
CPSIA information can be obtained
at www.ICGtesting.com
LVHW081748031123
762986LV00046B/1071

9 781505 820270